M000281497

STRETCHED

not

Broken

A Caregiver's Toolbox for Reducing & Managing Stress

Carol L. Rickard, LCSW

Founder of Well YOUniversity®

To get a dose of **motivation** & **inspiration** go to:

www.ThePowerofWordsEquote.com

Fill in your name & email!

STRETCHED *not* Broken:
A Caregivers Toolbox for Reducing & Managing Stress

by Carol L Rickard, LCSW

Well YOUniversity® Publications,
a DBA of WellYOUniversity, LLC
888 Life Tools

What will you get out of this book?

- Simple tools for making life easier.

- Being better able to manage stress, *rather than* stress manage you!

- Improved quality of life!

Contents

To get a dose of *motivation* & *Inspiration* go to:

www.ThePowerofWordsEquote.com

Fill in your name & email!

WHY I Wrote This Book!

The inspiration to write this 📖 came after I recently attended a NAMI Caregivers Conference.

The speaker was *excellent!*

She was dynamic, motivational, and inspirational.....

Yet I was left feeling an important part was <u>missing:</u>

ACTIONABLE!

For over **25** years I've been working in hospital programs helping **1,000's** of people learn skills they can actually USE to *make a difference in their lives.*

Today, I want to share those 'insider secrets' with you!

You see, I believe that we **ALL** need

TOOLS *to help us manage* *life* -

I call them: **LifeTOOLS!**

A person should **NOT** *have to get so sick*

they end up in a hospital in order to learn them!

So this book is being written to do just that!

I want to help you fill your

BEFORE

you ever get so sick you find yourself hospitalized.

 As you will see, my life as a caregiver

started when I was VERY young.

I didn't have ***ANY*** TOOLS –

or at least ***any healthy*** tools!

My Story

My 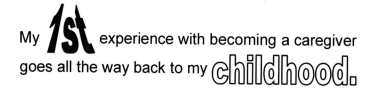 experience with becoming a caregiver goes all the way back to my childhood.

My father had cancer & died the end of my freshman year in high school.

I was just 14 years old at the time....

 My mother ended up getting VERY SICK just after that.

She actually had been given *'last rights'* twice.

Since my younger brother was at home – I became the person responsible for many things.

The roles between child & parent became reversed.

This included:

~ learning to drive **2 years** before legal age!

~ doing the  , cooking, &

~ making sure she took her medications
& got to her doctor's appointment.

I basically did most of the things
my mother *would have done*
had she only **been able to.**

So,

By the time I got to my senior year
I was ready for a change –
going to college gave me that change.

I guess you can say that I passed my
caregiver's torch off to my younger brother.

In **1987** I became my mother's caregiver again.

She was back in New Jersey, where she'd grown up,

& had to have **quadruple bypass surgery.**

However, this time, it was different.

I found myself feeling **grateful**

I was grateful being able to *give back* what I

knew she'd **given to me** *before my father died.*

Over the course of two years I once again cooked,

cleaned, shopped, & cared for my mother

until she lost her battle with cancer in 1989.

She'd been suffering from the pancreatic cancer,

 so I felt it was **a blessing** when

she **didn't have to suffer anymore.**

As you can see, I have some

experience with *life as a caregiver.*

While nobody's *situations* are the same.....

the **1thing** that does *stay the same*:

Being a caregiver can be *STRESSFUL...*

The tools I am about to share with YOU

I know they work.....

Not only have I been teaching them the past **25** years

I LIVE THEM EVERYDAY!

<u>NOTE</u>: I sometimes wish I'd learned them sooner!

However, *I know that God had a different journey*

planned for me so that I could be sitting here

writing them in this book FOR YOU!

About This Book

In my years of helping people successfully
change stress habits, I've reached a
conclusion I would like to share with you:

I believe people are *already smart enough*
when it comes to dealing with STRESS.

You KNOW WHAT TO DO!

It's the '*DOING*' or *lack of it* that
keeps you stuck where you are.

I can help *change* that!

I doubt you have read a   like this!
Unless, of course, you may have read
any of my **6** other books!

Along with **simple** & easy to understand chapters,

I tend to use a lot of pictures,

analogies

& word art

to make the information stick in the brain!

I call my approach:

SMARTheory™

It's what makes my books and services

different from all others!

KNOWLEDGE is the left brain at work.

This is where YOU *know* what to do!

Because I use "pictures" & "images", I end up

tapping in to the other side of the brain –

the right side!

This is also the side that synthesizes things,

like the operating system in a computer!

With both sides working on the 'same page',
the end result is getting people to

Move knowledge in to ACTION!

This book will introduce you to
proven tools for taking back
CONTROL of your L.I.F.E.

Up until NOW,
in order to get these 'insider secrets,
you'd have to get sick enough to
end up at the hospital.

That's WHY I am so excited
to be sharing them with you in this book!

Patients used to look at me like
I had a 3rd eye every time I said
they were *"lucky to end up in the hospital."*

Then I'd clarify –

I didn't mean lucky to get sick....

Lucky to be learning skills *EVERYONE needs*
to learn yet won't have the chance!

Today, YOU get an

opportunity to learn for yourself!

What this  *won't do:*

It **WILL NOT** give you 'the cure' to stress.

It **WILL NOT** get stress to 'go away'.

It **WILL NOT** give you 'a quick fix'.

It **WILL NOT** *even* give you 'a fix'.

It will give you back
a foundation for your life.

This foundation will give you the base needed
in order to be a caregiver & *live well today!!*

Getting Started!

Two birds are sitting on a wire.

One decides to fly away.

How many are left?

I like to start off my keynote speeches

with this little riddle.

It had such a tremendous impact on my life

the first time I heard it!

When they asked us to raise our hand

If we thought the answer was **one** -

My hand went up high & proud!

Wrong! The answer is two.

Oops!

DECIDING & DOING

are two different things!

Just because you decide to do something
DOESN'T mean that you DO it!

Now, I don't know about you –
But there had been plenty of times

In my life when I **Decided**

&

I *NEVER* FOLLOWED THRU!

(This little riddle *helped change that!*)

LifeTOOL #1

Direct

Opportunity

The same rule applies to this

If you don't use it, it *won't work*.

KNOWING & DOING
are two different things!

LifeTOOL #2

Denied

Opportunity

Not

'

Trying

Isn't it time you take charge

of the stress in *your LIFE?*

So let's get moving on to the tools
that can help you build the foundation for

L.I.F.E.

LifeTOOL #3   Here is my wordtool for life:

Living

Intentionally &

Fully

Engaged

It's In the Cards!

When you come to one of my live seminars,
one of the first things you will be handed
as you take your seat is a playing card!

It may be a king or it may be a three....

The key point is:

You **DON"T** get to **CHOOSE** what card you get!

This applies so wonderfully to LIFE –

where we are faced with many situations that

WE DON"T GET TO CHOOSE!

Like becoming a caregiver......

Instead,

we must work with what we're dealt!

As you know, I've been dealt some cards

I would have never chosen for myself.

Nonetheless, they became mine to play out!

As I look at history & even present times, I'm often inspired by people who have been dealt *such a rotten hand and yet triumph in spite of it!*

Sometimes when I am struggling or feeling **Sorry** for myself, I use other people's stories as a tool.

This brings me to:

LifeTOOL #4

This **LifeTOOL** I'd like to share with you can be found at the following web site:

www.SimpleTruths.com

Look for the Inspirational Movie Library

& click on "**FINISH STRONG.**"

I used to show this to my patients at least once a week! I recommend the same for you too!

PS. Simple Truths has many other great tools!

One of the most important messages of

Finish Strong:

WE *are responsible* for *making* **choices**.

LifeTOOL #5

> IT'S NOT
>
> *WHAT HAPPENS*
>
> TO YOU,
>
> BUT
>
> *HOW YOU REACT*
>
> TO IT
>
> **THAT MATTERS**
>
> EPICTETUS

Another way to think about it:

While we don't get to control the events in our lives,

We *do get to control* <u>our</u> <u>response</u> to them!

We either make our choice

or **it gets made for us!**

We are 100% responsible for our choice:

LifeTOOL #6

Controlling

How

Our

Intentions

Create

Experiences

© 2016 & licensed by Well YOUniversity, LLC
Taken from "Words At Work"

A few more tools:

LifeTOOL #7

> WHEN WE FACE A SITUATION
>
> THAT *CANNOT* BE CHANGED
>
> WE ARE **CHALLENGED**
> TO
> *CHANGE OURSELVES*
>
> VICTOR FRANKL

This is particularly useful since many

situations you will face as a caregiver

CANNOT be changed!

(More on this later..........)

LifeTOOL #8

THE CHOICES

YOU MAKE

MAKE YOU!

AUTHOR UNKNOWN

Got Tools?

Do you have a tool box  or a tool drawer in your home?

I'll bet money you have either **one or the other!**

Just as we have tools around to take care
of the 'physical' problems in our life,
we also need to have tools around to take care
of the 'emotional' problems in our life..

Now, I have another question for you!

Have you ever taken a knife and
tried to use it as a screwdriver?

Be honest!

(Usually when I ask this question in my workshops,
EVERYONE in the room raises their hands!)

How did it work?
Not *too* well, right?

At some point, we have to come back with
a real screwdriver and fix it again!

Now, just in case you are one of those people
who thinks the 'knife' worked just fine –

This question is for you!

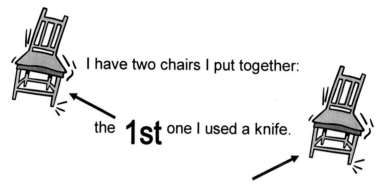

I have two chairs I put together:

the **1st** one I used a knife.

the **2nd** one I used a screwdriver.

Which chair do you want to sit in?!

I *thought so*..... the *screwdriver* chair!

One other thing!

What about -

Duct Tape

How many different things have you used this for?!

I remember one time being on a trip in college

where duct tape saved the day!

We were traveling from Manhattan, Kansas (Kansas

State University) to Kansas City for a concert.

The radiator hose sprung a leak!

Thank God we had some duct tape in the trunk....

We were able to get to there and back home again!

Duct Tape makes a great *temporary fix*

for a lot of different things

wouldn't you agree?!!

Let's face it though –

having the **'right tool'** for a job

can make all the difference

between **success** & failure.

I don't know about you....

I want to only have to do the job ONCE !

Survival Tools vs. LifeTools

  I believe the same kind of situation can happen when we are faced with 'emotional' problems.

We just grab at something quickly to help us deal with a situation,

I call these **Survival Tools**.

These are all the things we may have used to help us get through the tough times in life.

To help us **SURVIVE** ....

And in many instances,
they do help us – .**temporarily.**

The problem is that many of these

SURVIVAL TOOLS

go on to *become* a problem.

Let me share a couple of examples:

What you are looking at is a picture of one of my old
SURVIVAL TOOLS.

It was December 18, 1976 when I overheard the
conversation *I wasn't supposed to*. I **learned** my father
was dying from cancer. Remember, I was only 14,
just in my freshman year at Yosemite High School.

Now, **I didn't tell anyone** what I had heard...

Instead, I started *stealing liquor* from my parents.
We had just sold a bar & restaurant so there was
PLENTY of alcohol for me to get my hands on.

Also, my parents were busy dealing with my father so
no one noticed if anything was missing.

The truth be told, if my family had known how much I'd
been drinking – I know I would have been put in rehab.

Luckily for me, drinking

did not stay my survival tool.

Became my **LIFETOOL!**

You could find me on a court somewhere

shooting for hours on end

&

the drinking came to a stop.

Unfortunately, in May of 1977,

I had a new **SURVIVAL TOOL** emerge –

It was 6:00 o'clock in the morning on May 2, 1977.

I had just woken up & was on my way down the hallway

to get ready for school when my Mom stopped me.

As she told me I wouldn't be going to school today

because *my father had just passed away*, I remember

wrapping my arms around her and saying "It'll be okay."

My world instantly changed........

In that moment, which I can recall as if it were

yesterday, I also remember making

<u>a very conscious decision -</u>

I would just go on with my life as if my father had

never been there to begin with.....

This was my way of **SURVIVING** all the emotions that

would come along with such a great loss

I flipped my emotions switch OFF.

It stayed my **SURVIVAL TOOL** for a very long time.

It wasn't until my early **30**'s that I realized what had once helped me **SURVIVE** was now interfering with my life and preventing me from **LIVING**.

It ruined a lot of different relationships over the years.

It started to interfere with a *very important relationship.*

I had a choice: keep on not dealing with my emotions in a very healthy way or change & learn a new way!

 I didn't want to lose the relationship, so I started seeing a therapist for counseling.

I think of counseling as sort of a way to
learn more about yourself.

We don't know what we don't know!

Sometimes we need help from an objective party, outside our family and friends, to help guide us in the discovery to learn more about ourselves.

(I didn't realize the **connection** between my relationship problems & the emotion switch **until** I was in therapy!)

What I came to learn is:

Emotions are just like coins –

There are

2 sides to them & they can't be

separated!

In order to FEEL joy, love, happiness....

we must also feel sadness, anger, & pain

With my emotion switch back on

life has become much richer!!

ON

Instead of **AVOIDING** emotions,

We just have to learn how to **MANAGE THEM!**

And that was the beginning of my search for

LIFETOOLS

There is one more example of **SURVIVALTOOLS**

I want to talk about –

We all know who this is!

It is no secret that Oprah struggled
with her weight for many years...

I remember seeing her, in 1988, come out on her show
wearing those really *skinny* jeans,
pulling a wagon behind her
which represented all the weight she lost.

The success lasted one day!

It took her many more years to figure out <u>the secret</u>:
she used food as a way of coping with emotions!

I hope by now you begin to have a clearer picture of
what **SURVIVAL TOOLS** are &

why we need to swap them out for LIFETOOLS!

What do you use as YOUR **SURVIVALTOOL**?

Here are some examples of **SURVIVAL TOOLS**.

Do any of them sound familiar?!

Drinking

Spending

Food

 Work

Self Harm

Substance use

Keeping to yourself

Jokes & Humor   Being too independent

Relationships

Sex

Prescription drugs

Caretaking

 Being Angry

(and the list could go on!)

A very important point here is:

ANYTHING can be used as a **SURVIVAL TOOL!**

The things above can be *important parts* of our lives.

The difference becomes when we **USE** them

for **avoid situations in our lives** !

Keys to Changing Your Tools!

 **#1**

YOU are the one who must decide….

If what you're doing in life is working or not?

No one can answer this for you!

The fact remains that no matter what someone else tells us or how hard they try to get us to **change**….

We must make the decision ourselves!

Otherwise,

change will be very short-lived

IF it happens at all!

Steven Covey says it best:

"The gate of CHANGE
can only be opened from the inside"

 # 2

It is important not to *invalidate* the old tools....

I think it is very important **NOT** to beat yourself up over past behaviors. It doesn't matter if your old tools have been food, alcohol, drugs, sex, work, or anything else

I believe it is also very important to validate
the fact these old **SURVIVAL TOOLS**
helped us do just that: **SURVIVE**

I am where I am today because those early **SURVIVAL TOOLS** were a part of my life. Instead of looking at them with guilt & shame, I see them for what they were: **some things I 'grabbed at' to help get me through the VERY difficult times in my life**

Simply put – they are tools that I no longer choose because I have healthier ones I can use!

 **# 3**

YOU are the only one….

One of my mentor's, the late Jim Rohn has a great line:

"You can't pay somebody else
to do your push-ups for you!"

I hate to break the news to you –

<u>We</u> are the only ones that can make these changes!

In order to be successful,

We must take **100%** responsibility!

&

We must DO
what we DON"T FEEL LIKE DOING!

 **# 4**

Watch out for the COMFORT ZONES!!

One of the greatest challenges of change
is that we are
comfortable with what we know.

We must be on the lookout & notice when
we are going back to our old 'comfort zones".

Trust me, **this WILL happen**!

The key is to be on the **lookout** for it,
recognize it is happening, and
then take action to *get ourselves back on track!*

I love the exercise we do in my presentations that helps
people to experience this for themselves. I learned it in
a training from Jack Canfield, one of the authors of the
"Chicken Soup for The Soul" series.
Here's how it goes!

Put your hands together in front of you, interlocking your fingers. (like the picture!) Use your elbows to hold the book open!!

Now, whatever thumb you have on top, re-do your fingers so that your opposite thumb is now on top!

Go ahead and do it now!
How does it feel?

At first, it will feel kind of **uncomfortable!**

You may be *tempted* to go right back to the other way, which feels <u>more</u> <u>comfortable</u>.

Go ahead & resist the urge & hold them in this position!
You will notice it starts to feel a little less weird!
Hold it even longer and it will actually

start to feel more comfortable.

This is a great way to reinforce what happens to us when we try to make changes in our lives.

It FEELS UNCOMFORTABLE!

We have to keep practicing the new behavior so
we start to establish a new comfort zone!

 #5

Don't let FEAR stop you!

Besides the natural tendency to want to
stay in our comfort zones, there's one other
<u>HUGE</u> stumbling block to making change:

It is said we are born with **TWO** fears:

1) the fear of falling

2) the fear of loud noises

and all the others we learn.
Which means we can UNLEARN!

Breaking Through Fear

There are several **LIFETOOLS** I teach
to help my patients bust through fear
&
make healthy changes in their lives.

I would like to share them with you!
(These are the very same tools I live by!)

LifeTOOL #9

WORDS
CAN BE **POWERFUL,**

PUT IN TO *ACTION*

THEY BECOME

LIFE CHANGING!

CAROL L RICKARD

LifeTOOL #10

If you always do
what you've always done,

You'll always get
what you've always gotten,

Because if nothing changes...

NOTHING CHANGES!

Author Unknown

I had a patient teach this to me!

She'd ended up back in the hospital

for the 3rd time in just a couple months.

The last time I saw her
she pulled out a piece of paper
& this saying was written on it!

Needless to say, I haven't see her anymore since then!

LifeTOOL #11

One of the best books I ever read

that helped me **really learn** to manage my fears:

"Who Moved My Cheese"
by Dr. Spencer Johnson.

If you haven't read this, I strongly recommend it!

It is a short story, about 90 pages long,
about these little characters who live in a maze
and are forced to deal with change.

It can be a **LIFE CHANGER!**

You'll have to look for the book in
the *business section*.

However,

it truly is more of a Life Lesson's story!

LifeTOOL #12

It was during the first time I played an audio version
of **"Who Moved my Cheese"** for my patients
when I came up with this next tool.

I was sitting there, thinking about how to help people
see change in a different way so they would welcome &
embrace it rather than be afraid of it. I came up with:

Creating

Healthy

And

New

Growth

Experiences

© 2016 & licensed by Well YOUniversity, LLC
Taken from "Words At Work"

This was the first "Word At Work" of many to come!

LifeTOOL #13

Feel the fear and do it anyway!

This is the title of *another great book*,

"Feel the Fear and Do It Anyway" - Dr. Susan Jeffries

It becomes a great tool when you put it in to practice!

LifeTOOL #14

Recognize that fear is really our brain *playing a trick* on us! It may help you to look at fear in the following way:

Find

Emotion

Alters

Reality

© 2016 & licensed by Well YOUniversity, LLC
Taken from "Words At Work"

LifeTOOL #15

This next strategy is another one I
learned from a Jack Canfield training:

You can do this either standing or sitting.
*Pinch your thumb and 1st or 2nd finger together
on both hands.*

Hold them out in front and to the sides of you.

Now repeat this mantra in a low 'hum':

"Oh what the heck,
go for it anyways"

(If you don't want to make a scene,
duck in to the bathroom!)

I love this strategy!!!!! One of my favorites!

It's a great way to break through
the old fear recording that plays in our head!

I think it works so great because
it combines **the mind & the body**...

47

Why Wellness?

HOW MANY CARS HAVE YOU OWNED?

or

HOW MANY HAVE BEEN IN YOUR HOUSEHOLD?

(This includes new & used ones!)

1

3

5

Maybe More!

(Depending on your age of course!)

Imagine….

You had 1 car that had to last you a lifetime.

How well would you take care of that car?!

If you are like most people,

you would probably take very good care of it,

including regular *preventive* maintenance!

Well, I *love* to be the one to break the news to you…

We **ONLY** get one vehicle to *live our life with!*

ONE BODY that has to
LAST A LIFETIME!

What is Wellness?

Wellness is the key to having

this **one body be able to last us a lifetime!**

For many years, I used to define it as

"optimal health".

I liked the definition because <u>not</u> <u>everyone's</u> the same.

Some years ago, as I was preparing

for a speech, I came across the

BEST definition.

I love to share it with others!

<u>The National Wellness Institute's:</u>

"Wellness is an *active process* of *becoming*

aware of & *making choices* towards

a *MORE* successful existence."

I'd like to break this down & take a look at each of the key pieces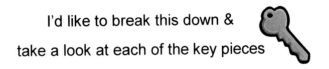

<u>active process</u>

WE must take some kind of action.

WELLNESS *doesn't happen* by ACCIDENT!

This means you & I must take responsibility

& DO STUFF!

One of the secrets I've learned over the past 25 years is *even* a little action works!

HAVE you ever saved pennies, nickels, dimes, & quarters? Then you know!

They seem like such small amounts –

especially the pennies nickels & dimes!

Yet, they can ADD UP!

We'll talk about 'making changes' in a later chapter.

I have some secrets to share with you!

Here is my wordtool for action:

LifeTOOL #16

A

Critical

Task

Implemented

Only

Now!

<u>becoming aware of</u>

What you're doing at this very moment,

just by reading this book!

By keeping an open ear & an open mind

you have taken the 1st step.

When we say:

"That won't work for me."

"That has nothing to do with me."

"How could that possibly work?"

We are not keeping an open mind….

Be on the lookout

Don't let your mind **sneak shut** on you

AT ANY TIME!

You don't have to **AGREE with everything.**

You DO have to **_BE OPEN to everything!_**

One other critical step is to start

becoming aware of your behaviors.

Are there things you are currently either

DOING or NOT DOING

that are keeping you stuck?

This means taking an honest look at WHAT

you're doing & answering the following:

IS
This
HELPING
ME?

OR

IS
THIS
HURTING
ME?

<u>making choices</u>

NOBODY chooses to get sick or have an illness.

And yet, we *must choose to be well.*

The choices we make TODAY make
a difference in moving us towards either:

or

Illness   **Wellness**

Many times it *may seem like*

we **don't even** have a choice.....

This can happen when we don't like **any**
of the options we have to choose from.

Don't be fooled by this!

Just because we *may not like the options,*

Doesn't mean that we shouldn't choose!

<u>more successful existence</u>

I LOVE that *this applies to EVERYONE!*

So if symptoms never go away completely,

Or

An illness just gets worse over time -

a person can always
AIM to have a

"successful existence"

And most importantly,

What that is for one person

doesn't mean

it has to be for EVERYONE.

This definition provides the HOPE that we can have

illness & wellness at the SAME TIME!

Stress Management Made Simple

"Raise your hand if you know STRESS is BAD for your health?"

When I ask this question in my speaking – everyone in there will raise their hand! I'm sure you too would also raise your hand! So we can stop here, right?   *WRONG!*

Even though we all *know* **STRESS** is *BAD for us*, very few people do anything about it!

Remember, I like to take a different approach & help people **DO** something about it!

After all, if we can reduce our **STRESS** levels, we can actually keep the one vehicle, our **BODY**, **running & lasting a whole lot longer!**

I want you to get a piece of paper & pen right now, before you go to the next page.

Don't go there until you have them ready!

What do you think of when you see this?

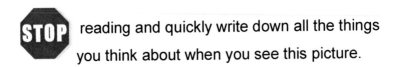 reading and quickly write down all the things you think about when you see this picture.

When you are done writing, let's continue!

I love doing this exercise! What I find is that each person usually has something different come to mind when they see or hear the word **STRESS**.

When I do this exercise in a workshop,
we get a lot of different answers.

I'd like to share some of them with you!

They may be very similar to what you've written down.

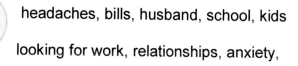 headaches, bills, husband, school, kids

looking for work, relationships, anxiety,

loss of control, can't sleep, shopping,

break up, family, job interviews, money,

birthdays, not working, overwhelmed, life, tuition,

kid's schedules, holidays, Dr.'s appointments, driving

Now here is an important part for you to understand:

What is STRESS?

"A response to a situation or change."

Let's talk about "response" for a moment.

Usually the response is something we don't

have much control over

once it starts.

Kind of like a reflex –
the doctor hits my knee and my leg moves!

Has this ever happened to you?

You have a big event going on in your life.

Let's say an interview for a job.

First off, you don't sleep very well the night before.

Then as you are getting ready,

your stomach starts to twist and turn.

You are about to have a case of the 'runs'!

Now, who would *actually let these responses happen*?

 NO ONE!

This is the thing about STRESS –

Once it rolls, we <u>don't</u> <u>get</u> <u>to</u> <u>have</u> too much control!

Before we move on, I also want to point out
something else that is VERY important:

STRESS does not come one size fits all!

Here's what I mean by this:

1st we must realize that 'the change or situation' does not always come in a negative form!

We can have **POSITIVE**

changes or situations that can trigger a response.

Look at your list:

Can you identify some POSITIVE stress sources on it?

If you didn't write any down,

can you think of any right now that you could add?

2nd we must realize 'the change or situation' does not come in just one size!

It can be either BIG or SMALL.

Think about it for a moment.....

What happens to your stress level when the kids are

running 5 minutes late in the morning?

or

You are running 5 minutes late for an appointment?

3rd we must realize **'the change or situation'** may be stressful for one person but *not another*!

STRESS is a very **personal thing!**

Just because something may not be *STRESS to me* does not mean it *may not be STRESS to you!*

I wanted to share with you one of my
POSITIVE STRESSES!

Now that we have a little clearer picture of STRESS

LET"S DO SOMETHING ABOUT IT!!

Do you have kids?

Has your washer ever been broken?

Do you hate to do laundry?

If you answered YES to any of the above,
then you already may be a bit of a
stress expert & not even know it!

This is the pile of laundry after just 1 week!

Heading in to the next week, things are so busy

that you don't have any time to do laundry.

It has to **wait** until next weekend.

This is the pile of laundry you are looking at week 2!

It starts to GROW BIGGER!!

But wait…..

There just isn't enough time to get it all done.

You've got the kid's conference this week,

it's your mother's birthday, and

you still have to go shopping for a present.

Everyone has enough clothes to last them

one more week…..

Besides, there isn't anything happening next weekend.

So......laundry is put off for another week!

Imagine **how** you would **feel** if you had to look

at a pile of laundry as tall as you?!

What can we do to *keep laundry from piling up*?

Do a load as frequently as possible!

Sometimes we may need to do **2 loads or more** a day!

STRESS is just like laundry!

It piles up!

Sure!

You can *pretend* it's not there!

Maybe even try to hide it!

Whether you see it or not –

it still keeps *piling up*!

LifeTOOL #17

Do **at least** one load a day of

Stress Laundry!

[This *means you must select and do at least one of the activities listed in the following pages. Don't rely on the same one or two. Try things you've never done before!*]

STRESS AWAY
LAUNDRY SOAP

Guaranteed to lighten any day!

Directions:

* Use at least one time daily.

* Separate in to piles if
   too large for one load.

* May need to do multiple loads!

Bake · Draw · Hot shower or bath · Clean · Play a game! · Cook · Do laundry · Call a friend · Use Serenity Prayer · Spend time alone · Mow the lawn · Say "no" · Volunteer · Exercise · Meditate · Read · Chop wood · Organize: make a schedule or a "to do" list · Zoo · Hobbies · Plan a trip · Spend time with a pet · Visit someone · Movies · Shopping Mall · Go to a park · Water Plants · Puzzles: Jigsaw or Word · Gardening · Ask for help · Write a letter · Do your nails · Listen to music · Take a walk · Crafts · Support group · Go for a drive · Constructive Destruction! · Guided Imagery · Library · Punch a pillow · Sports: watch play · Treat yourself · Work on the car · Play cards · Paint: pictures walls · Sing along with the radio · Picnic · Start a journal · Wash the car · Deep Breathing · Go out to dinner · Try something new! · Flea Market · Play Loungeball! · Have a manicure

71

LifeTOOL #18

Avoid adding to the PILE!

Take steps to **AVOID** the things that cause you STRESS!

Only when I started doing my own laundry did I come to appreciate why my Mom would get so mad when I would change clothes a bunch!!

LifeTOOL #19

If it doesn't involve you

Don't get involved!

Carol L Rickard

LifeTOOL #20

S + T = R

Situation   Thinking   Response

This equation is a **powerful tool** if put in to practice!

Let me share a personal example of this put to work:

One spring a few years ago, I was catching a flight back to Philadelphia from San Jose, California.

I was waiting at the gate for my flight when I **suddenly realized** the jacket I was going to need once I got to Philly was packed in the _suitcase that got checked_.

 What made the situation WORSE was that my car key was in my jacket pocket!

Now my immediate thought was "I'm in trouble!"
(since we know how often suitcases don't arrive!)

My next thought was "I can't do anything about it now!"

And I went back to enjoying the NBA Playoff game!

SITUATIONS will **HAPPEN**

What we **CHOOSE TO THINK** is the difference maker:
migraine & no migraine!
stressed out or relaxed!

As you can see, when it comes to **STRESS**
most people familiar with laundry are already experts!
Okay, maybe not the person who takes everything
to the dry cleaners!

It makes sense, doesn't it?

We all have to do

a little stress laundry everyday!

PS. I wanted to share some of the other ways
I **avoid** adding to my pile of **STRESS**:

#1) When I have to go someplace new for a speech
or an appointment, I'll go find it ahead of time. or

I make sure to leave myself extra time to find it.

#2) I plan out my meals for the week & **avoid** the

STRESS of coming home from work &

trying to figure out 'what's for dinner?'

#3) At work, I **avoid** the **STRESS** of not getting things

done by making sure I complete what I'm

working on, before I move on to the next!

(This really use to be a **very big STRESS**, as I had this

habit of skipping around to different tasks &

then feeling like I wasn't accomplishing anything!)

#4) I make sure I get my exercise done each **morning**

This way it's done and I don't have to worry

about still doing it later when I get home from work!

However, there are those times when things pile up.

Times in LIFE when we seem to get **DUMPED ON**.

I refer to this as

"The Dump Truck O'Stress"

Let me illustrate this next!

Dump Truck O'Stress!

- - - - -

A truck full of 'dirty laundry was
suddenly dropped on your front door...

How would you **FEEL?**   What would you **DO?**

Here are some pretty natural reactions:

Angry	Give Up
Overwhelmed	Explode
Powerless	Hide
Hopeless	Run

Life's big STRESS cause the *same reactions* –

These are life events & changes that come on
quickly, without warning, and in a big way

**The equivalent of a dump truck
full of dirty laundry!**

LifeTOOLS #21-27

What to do when the Dump Truck O'Stress pulls up:

1. Give yourself permission to **feel the way you do** (Otherwise it just adds to the pile!)

2. Break it in to **smaller piles**
(Small piles are easier to manage!)

3. Ask for **help** (The more people working on a pile, the better the chance of getting through it!)

4. Make a plan or a **time schedule**
(This helps keep you focused!)

5. Prioritize
(Figure out what's important to take care of first)

6. Be **realistic**!
(It may take a while to chip away at the pile)

7. Take it **"one pile at a time"**
(This makes less stress!)

I want to come back to something I think
A LOT of people struggle with:

Starting projects & tasks but not finishing them!

I mentioned it earlier as part of my old work stress but
it used to happen a lot around the house too:

clean clothes waiting to get put away...

the basement only half way cleaned up...

phone calls I was going to make & never did..

I used to get more frustrated because
I couldn't seem to get anything done!

That was until I came upon this next **LIFETOOL**!

I actually started thinking about the word "finish" for
my patients. If I could just help them be able to
follow through and finish things!

Well, I myself have been using this tool with great
success over the past couple months....

I wanted to make sure to share it with you!

LifeTOOL #28

It's simple to use –

When you start a task or a project,

you must **keep repeating** the word

&

it's "At Work" saying!

Focus

In

Now

Instead

Stopping

Halfway

Managing Emotions

All Shook Up

Has this ever happened to you?
  You go into a store & buy either a liter of
    diet coke or some raspberry seltzer.

Along the way, you are very careful not to shake it up!

Then one evening that next week,

you go to pour yourself a glass,

your mind busy paying attention to dinner on the stove

and ....

SPLASH.......

stuff comes flying out of the bottle you just opened -
all over you & the floor creating a mess!

Sometimes in life,

  it doesn't matter how careful we are.

    Things will still get shaken up!

I believe the same thing happens

when it comes to our emotions!

Sometimes **WE** get *shaken up!*

And if we aren't careful,

WE end up with a **BIG EMOTIONAL MESS!**

If we are to have any success at moving away from
using **SURVIVAL TOOLS** as a way of
coping with our emotions,

then

we have got to learn a little more about

managing them in a healthy way!

I want to introduce you to my system I call

"The Feeling's Pendulum".

Take a look at the next page
& see where you would put yourself!

The Feelings Pendulum

What Do You Do

With Your Feelings?

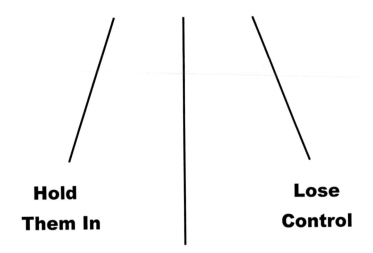

**Hold
Them In**

**Lose
Control**

**Manage
Them**

So which one did you pick?

If you are a "Manage Them", congratulations!

You obviously know what to do with your emotions!

If you are a "Hold Them In",

I am going to guess at times, you also can "Lose It"!

Finally, if you start at "Lose Control", & stay at

"Lose Control", **don't worry**! Help is on the way!

I like using a pendulum because it

perfectly illustrates just how difficult can be to

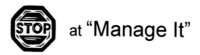 at "Manage It"

if you start up on either end.

Momentum makes it difficult to stop!

I have another way I like to teach people to

think about emotions and how to manage them!

First, let me ask:

"Have you ever said something

 you wished had *never*

come out of your mouth?"

I think most people can relate to experiences like this!!!

Here's why it happens –

When our emotions are so high that their level
is up to our nose – simply by opening our mouth
to speak they will come SPILLING OUT!

When things are at this high of a level –
we will have **NO CONTROL** over what comes out!

Best not to say anything when emotions are this high!
WAIT! There's an even worse level to be at....

BRAIN LEVEL!

When we are filled with emotion up above our 's

we lose control over our brain!

It's like our brain gets **"flooded"** & we can end up

DOING STUPID THINGS,

not just saying them!

[Okay, maybe this hasn't happened to you. But I am

sure you can think of other people this might describe!]

I have a simple process I teach my patients I call

Carol's Two Steps to Success!

Step 1) **STOP** the level from rising any higher.

Step 2) **RELEASE** so that the level will drop.

IMPORTANT:

It is only when the level is *lower* than the neck,

that we should attempt to talk!

If our emotion is right at neck level it'll *still* **CHOKE US!**

STOP the Level From Rising!

There are many ways to **STOP** our level of emotions from rising. Remember, there are both healthy AND unhealthy ways!

Think of **SURVIVAL TOOLS** vs. **LIFETOOLS!**

Some **unhealthy** ways: (SURVIVAL TOOLS)

Eat   Drink   Sleep   Shut down   Isolate

Avoidance   Become numb   Ignore things

Self-harming behaviors   Use negative self-talk

Some *healthy* ways: LifeTools #29-47

Take a time out   Belly Breathing   Count to 10

Set limits   Decline to talk about it anymore

Guided Imagery   Consider the Source   Listen to music

Use the Serenity Prayer   Walk Away

Focus on something else   Use **+** self-talk

Change your thought pattern   meditation   prayer

'It is what it is'   All passive relaxation techniques

Decline the invitation to fight   walk outside & look UP!

RELEASE So the Level Will Drop

In order to **release emotion**……

muscle involvement is required.

Think of it like we are bailing water out of a boat.

We must take ACTION

in order to get the water out!

The same principle applies to emotions.

We must take ACTION to get the emotion out!

It requires we involve 'muscles'

to actually **create the release**!

The quick 3 to remember: LifeTOOLS #48-50

Walk	Talk	Write!

If you remember nothing more than these & put them in to practice, you will be on your way to *managing your emotions rather than having them manage you!*

PS. You can also use the many more active releases

from our chapter on stress!

After all, emotions can often be *our response to stress!*

In my workshops, I will take a couple liter bottles

& hand them out to different people to

shake them up really good.

I want to use them to reinforce a point

about managing emotions.......

Our **emotions** are just like the pressure that builds up

inside those bottles when they get " **ALL SHOOK UP!**"

It doesn't do any good to simply **STOP** the shaking!!!!!

We must also create the release!!!

Think about it for a moment.

What happens if someone takes a bottle that's

been **"ALL SHOOK UP!"** & sets it

back in the refrigerator or in the cupboard?

The pressure doesn't go anywhere!!!!!
UNTIL....

it just ends up dumping a mess on
the next unsuspecting person!

The same happens with our emotions....

We end up **dumping them out on the next person**!

To prevent this from happening we

MUST USE A RELEASE!

(Kind of like when you take a bottle and twist the cap a little bit at a time to let some of the pressure out!)

There is another **IMPORTANT** point to remember....

We can't often tell just by looking at the bottle whether or not it has any pressure built up inside!

Just as we often can't tell looking at a person whether or not they have any emotional pressure built up inside!!!

The best strategy is PREVENTION! Approach with **caution** & be prepared to **move quickly** out of the way!

LifeTOOL #51

This next **LIFETOOL** is something
that is required if you are to have
long term success at managing your emotions!

Once again, I had a patient that I was working with
who was having so much difficulty just
knowing WHAT she was feeling!

The word came to me rather quickly! Again, I know this
is a great tool because it is another one I use regularly!

Actively

Work

At

Recognizing

Existences

The Power Tools!

WHETHER YOU THINK YOU CAN

OR

YOU THINK YOU CAN'T...

YOU'RE RIGHT!

HENRY FORD

Brain Power

One of the most powerful tools we have is our brain!

The *problem* for most people is they have theirs working **AGAINST** them instead of FOR them.

The previous quote says it all!
I believe it was written by Henry Ford.
(*I'm not certain as I have heard it many different times!*)

Think about it for a moment......

There are so many great inventors like Henry Ford, the Wright Brothers, & Thomas Edison who **thought they could**, even when *the world thought they couldn't.*
In fact, the world believed it impossible!

They learned to harness their brain's power to work FOR THEM allowing their dreams come to life!.

I wonder?

What dreams would you achieve if
you believed **YOU COULD!!!!!!**

This is my example of:

"If you think you can or
you think you can't,
You're right"

This is Half Dome, located in *Yosemite National Park*. This is a view that **most** of the park's millions of visitors each year will **NEVER** see.....

In order to get where this picture was taken, you have to hike **8 miles** in to the *back country* of Yosemite.

Of course, it's all up hill! It ends up rising from 4,000 foot elevation in the valley to 8,800 feet at the top.

My brother & I had reached the bottom of the dome. I can't repeat exactly what he said, but a clean translation is "Holy Shit!" At that moment our thoughts of climbing to the top vanished! However, we felt very proud of our accomplishment just getting to here!

We thought WE CAN'T!

My nieces unexpectedly showed up! We thought they were ahead of us & half way up the dome by now! Excited & eager for us to **ALL** reach the top, they encouraged us to give it a try. After all, we had come this far.....

They got us thinking WE CAN!

And we did!

This is the view from the top!

Yosemite Valley is down below!

I don't know who the guy was!
I just thought he was brave.

What are YOU stopping yourself from doing?!

A Life Changed

It comes as quite a shock to my patients & colleagues
I *was once* the **most negative, pessimistic person.**

I didn't think anything could go my way.

I was working **12** hours a day and

still barely paying my bills.

I made **less** at my job than what I paid to go to college.

For me, there was *nothing good about anything.*

But then in 1989 I had a moment that was life changing.
I will share more about this in a moment. Since then,
I've tried to learn as much as I can about using the
power of thoughts as a tool for transformation &
wellness. My study has impacted both my personal and
professional life. As I learn new ideas & strategies, I try
to incorporate them not only in to my life but also in to
my work with others. After all, what good is knowledge
if it is not shared! I'm on a mission to share
what I have learned with others!

I'm thankful for the opportunity to share it with you.

I had mentioned earlier that I had a moment in 1989
which changed my life around.

It was a blessing hidden in heart ache.

&

has truly shaped the life I live today.

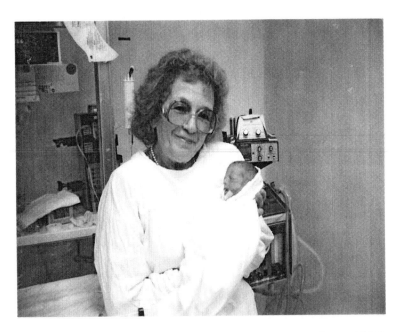

This is a picture of my mother taken December, 1988.
She is holding my nephew, Christopher.

It is my mother who gave me
the greatest gift a person could receive.
Let me explain…..

My mother had called me at work to tell me her doctor wanted her to come in to the hospital right away. It was only when we got in to a room at the emergency room my mother finally told me about the cancer.

It is *no surprise* she had kept this information to herself. After all, she'd done it before!!

That afternoon I was on the phone with my sisters out in California making plans to get my mother out West so she could have a chance to see everyone.

Those plans never happened........

My mother ended up passing away that very night. With the tears, sadness, grief and heartache came the greatest gift I could ever receive:

It doesn't matter what we plan for tomorrow ~
We must live our life today as if it were the only one.

We must live One Day At A Time

LifeTOOL #53

I have an exercise I created & I'd like to share with you.

First, read the following:
YESTERDAY, TODAY, and TOMORROW

There are two days in every week that we need not worry about, two days that must be kept free from fear and apprehension.

One is **YESTERDAY**, with it's mistakes & cares, it's faults & blunders, it's aches & pains. Yesterday has passed, forever beyond our control. All the money in the world cannot bring back yesterday. We cannot undo a single   act we performed. Nor can we erase a single word we've said – Yesterday is gone!

The other day we must not worry about is **TOMORROW**, with it's impossible adversaries, it's burden, it's hopeful promise and poor performance. Tomorrow is beyond our control!

Tomorrow's sun will rise either in splendor or behind a mask of clouds – but it will rise. And until it does, we have no stake in tomorrow, for it is yet unborn.

This leaves only one day – **TODAY**. Any person can fight the battles of just one day. It is only when we add the burdens of yesterday & tomorrow that we break down.

It is not the experience of today that drives people mad—it is the remorse of bitterness for something which happened yesterday, and the dread of what tomorrow may bring.   LET US LIVE ONE DAY AT A TIME!!!!

(Author Unknown)

Second, take a blank piece of paper and
write Yesterday, Tomorrow, & Today on it
so it looks like this:

```
┌─────────────────────────────────┐
│                                 │
│           Yesterday             │
│                                 │
│                                 │
│                                 │
│           Tomorrow              │
│                                 │
│                                 │
│                                 │
│            Today                │
│                                 │
│                                 │
│                                 │
│                                 │
│                                 │
└─────────────────────────────────┘
```

Under "Yesterday" -

I want you to write down all the things from **the past**
(from yesterday or 20 years ago) that still occupy your
thoughts. This includes regrets, resentments, hurts,
the I shoulda-woulda-coulda's, guilt's, & anything else!

Under "Tomorrow" -

I want you to write down all the things from **the future** that occupy your thoughts. This includes worries, fears, "what-if's", uncertainties, hopes, & dreams!

Under TODAY -

I want you to look back over the things you've written under yesterday & tomorrow. Ask yourself this **?** about *each* of the items you have listed:

"Is there anything I can **DO** about that TODAY?"

If there is, write down under **TODAY** the **SPECIFIC ACTION** you can take.

It must be something you can DO!

If there isn't,
don't write anything under TODAY

Once you have completed this,
there is one last step to take!

Fold the paper *just above* where **TODAY** is written.

Now, keep folding it back & forth several times on that same crease. You can even lick it if you want but don't get a paper cut!

Now carefully tear the paper
along the crease.

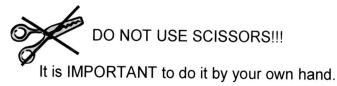 DO NOT USE SCISSORS!!!

It is IMPORTANT to do it by your own hand.

You should end up with 2 pieces of paper in your hands.

One piece has <u>Yesterday</u> & <u>Tomorrow</u> on it.

Feel free to burn this, rip it up, shred it, and destroy it!

The other piece has TODAY on it.

Hold onto this!

It is the only day we **CAN** DO anything about.

You may need to do repeat this every day until you're able to focus on TODAY!

Other ways of looking at it:

LifeTOOL #54

'WHY'S'

GET US LOST IN THE PAST

'WHAT-IF'S'

GET US LOST IN THE FUTURE

CAROL L RICKARD

Are these words you often speak?

If so, they will prevent you from

Living in Today!

LifeTOOLS #55 & 56

YOU CAN'T REWRITE THE PAST

HOWEVER,

YOU HOLD THE PEN
TODAY!

CAROL L RICKARD

The

Only

Day

Afforded

You!

LifeTOOL #57

Another *powerful* **LIFETOOL** for me has long been the **Serenity Prayer**. I started putting it in to practice in my life after I started working an addictions treatment unit.

I had heard of & was familiar with it; however it wasn't until I was around people who could teach me how to USE IT, that it became one of my primary tools.
Just like 'One Day at a Time' - this **LIFETOOL** holds

The Power of Peace & Serenity

My strongest test of this tool came in the summer of 2006. It was in July when my sister Kris suddenly died.

Since I live in central New Jersey, I flew out of Philadelphia. My flight got out of the gate right on time....but once on the way to the runway; we sat there for almost **2** hours.

I was to catch a connecting flight out of Salt Lake City in to Reno. My brother & his family, flying from

Virginia, were on the same flight out of Salt Lake City. Needless to say – I never caught up with them.

My delay in Philly had me miss the connecting flight. The worst news came when I was booked on a flight the next morning: **1 hour** after the funeral was to start. Now here I was stranded the night in Salt Lake City.

Really, what could I do? So, I kept the Serenity Prayer repeating in my head over & over & over again.

I called my family from the airport in Salt Lake City & informed them I wouldn't even be leaving Salt Lake City **until the next day and AFTER the funeral had already started.**

As I kept repeating the Serenity Prayer, I let the tears flow. I had a lot of mixed emotions and I knew it wasn't a good idea to hold them in.

In the past, under stressful conditions like these I would have had a major migraine before the plane ever landed in Utah.

Turns out, I didn't get a migraine all weekend.
This was despite not getting to my sister's house
until AFTER all the days events had taken place.
My **LIFETOOL** held me steady.

As I said a little earlier in this book, there are many
times in life we don't get to choose what happens.....

We *DO* get to *CHOOSE* our *RESPONSE* to them!

God grant me,

**The *Serenity* to accept the things
I cannot change**

The *Courage* to change the things I can

And the *Wisdom* to know the difference

LifeTOOL #58

Here is my shortened version of it:

Can I do anything about it
right now?

If not, I just have to **let it go!**

Important:

I would like to make this point about *'Letting Go'* or
as they say in recovery circles: *'Let go and let God'*

We cannot let go of something
we have not allowed
ourselves to feel!

In order to 'let go' of something –

we must first **FEEL the FEELINGS** connected to it

and then

'Let Go'!

(One way to think of this is we simply have something
come in through one ear, acknowledge it (feel it!),
and move on out through the other side!)

LifeTOOL #59

Another way I explain 'Let Go' to my patients:

Leave

Everything

To

Gods

Ownership

LifeTOOL #60

And one last way to practice "Letting Go"!

Write down what it is you are trying to

'let go' of on a small slip of paper.

Then do one of the following with the slip:

✶ Put it in a special box you have decorated
(Many people refer to these as a God Box
or a Worry Box. You can find all types of
boxes at your local craft store)

✶ Put it in a special book
(This could be a book of worship or
another special book of yours)

✶ Throw it in a fireplace
(If you don't have one, it could be any other
safe way to destroy it by burning!)

✶ Shred it up
(This could be as simple as throwing
it in the shredder or tearing it by hand
in to a bunch of little itty, bitty pieces!

You will notice the one thing these all have in common
is they **REQUIRE ACTION BE TAKEN!**
Instead of just trying to do this '*all in our head*',
we get our entire body involved in the process!

I believe it is this **PRINCIPLE OF DOING**
which leads us to great success.

When our mind starts to go back
to thinking about it again…..

Be prepared that it will!
Our mind <u>will</u> try to hold on to things!!

We can also remind ourselves we have "gotten rid"
of **what** it is trying to access again!

I have one more **LIFETOOL** I would like to share with
you that belongs here with **The Power Tools!**

It's on the next page -

LifeTOOL #61

The long version!

Giving

Respect

And

Thanks

Into

The

Usual

Daily

Experiences

Giving

Respect

And

Thanks

Everyday

For

Unbelievable

Life

LifeTOOL #63   **Grateful By the ½ Dozen!**
Everyday, either in the morning or at nighttime,
come up with 6 things you can be grateful for that day!

Tools

For Change

Changeology!

Over the past **25** years I've developed some great tools for making lasting change.

Did you know there are actually ways we can set ourselves up TO FAIL – *before we even start?*

Will power is one of those ways!
It *might* help us make *short lived change* –

However, it doesn't help us very much when we are trying to make **LASTING** change.

Willpower is like a battery! You can only use it for so long before it starts to weaken!

On to
Tools for CHANGE!

Tool # 1

*Focus on what you will **GAIN!***

Not on what you'll lose.

This is usually the **1st** place where people get it
wrong. They actually do the opposite!

"If I don't quit smoking, I could die"

*"If I don't lose this weight, the doctor
says I could have a heart attack or a stroke"*

*"I don't want to get fired so I better learn
this new computer program"*

Instead:

*"If I quit smoking, **I'll be able to walk Carol
down the aisle at her wedding!**"*

*"I want to be 40 pounds lighter **so I can
play ball with my grandson.**"*

*"By learning this new program, I am **making
myself more qualified for a better job!**"*

119

Tool # 2

START **SMALL!**

This is usually the **2nd** place people get it wrong!

Again, they tend to do the opposite!

Whatever the change is –

Break it down in to **baby steps 1**st

Exercise:

Start by walking during commercials.

Then go out for a 5 minute walk.

Slowly build up the time to 20-30 min.

 *If for some reason you*

DON'T *FEEL LIKE* doing it –

Make yourself **do just 1 min** & then **STOP!**

This way it continues **to build the momentum**

and won't slow your progress.

Tool # 3

Use an *anchor!*

Write the change you are making

on a small piece of paper or an index card.

It should be written in the following way:

In the *present tense,*

using only *positive language,*

& with *feeling attached!*

Examples:

*" I am so happy being able to
walk Carol down the aisle!"*

"I feel grateful I can now play ball with my grandson."

I am excited with having new job opportunities!"

Read it:

- ✓ **Wake up**
- ✓ **Before sleep**

This will help keep you "anchored" to the healthy changes you are In the process of making!

Again, here's my wordtool for change:

Creating

Healthy

And

New

Growth

Experiences

Tool # 4

CHANGE is a process!

It is something we aim at – like a target
but don't beat ourselves up if we miss!

Remember, learning anything *new* requires

practice for it to become a **NEW** habit.

This is WHY change is a process!!

Don't get discouraged when you find yourself
slipping back to old behaviors.
Learn from the 'slips' and move on.

2 steps forward, **1** step back
still has us *moving* CLOSER to **our goals.**

Try this exercise!

START on one side of a room.

Take TWO STEPS forward

&

ONE STEP **back.**

Now, do it again!

Take TWO STEPS forward

&

ONE STEP **back.**

Repeat this process at least *2 more times!*

Are you closer to the other side
of the room than where you started?

 YES!!!

So when your *brain* starts to YELL at you:

'you're going backwards'

Yell back! "No I'm not!!"

LifeTOOL #64

Here is my wordtool for: Practice

Purposely

Repeat

Activities

Critical

To

Improving

Core

Existence

Wrapping Things Up

We started off by taking a look at how we don't always get to choose what's **IN THE CARDS!!**

We are, however,

100% responsible for how we respond.

We then moved on to **"GOT TOOLS?"** It is important to remember we can USE many things **AS SURVIVAL TOOLS**. My hope is you now have:

a better understanding of your behaviors

&

instead of beating yourself up over them; to validate the important role they ONCE played in your life.

2 questions to now ask yourself:

Are any **SURVIVAL TOOLS** now hurting me?

If there are, the next question is:

Is it time for me to turn in my **SURVIVAL TOOLS?**

If the answer is **NO**, that's okay!

Now just may not be the time for you to do so.

We all have our own journey to take us
to a point where it is time to change.

As long as you are honest with yourself
& promise to re-visit this question,
I hold on to the hope that when the
time comes & you need to change,

YOU WILL!

If the answer is **YES**,

I hold on to the hope that you may now have enough
"LIFETOOLS' to get the job done!

Remember, learning anything new requires
practice for it to become a new habit.
Change is a process!!

Do not get discouraged should you find yourself
slipping back to old behaviors every now & then.

Learn from the 'slips' and move on.

LifeTOOL #65

Find

An

Important

Lesson

Using

Real

Experiences

Then we focused on
STRESS. MANAGEMENT MADE SIMPLE!

The goal here is to have gotten you thinking
differently about STRESS & seeing how easy
it is to do something about it!

Remember, the best way to stress less is
**DO A LOAD OF STRESS LAUNDRY
EVERDAY!**

As you become more aware of when it is
PILING UP,

You may need to do extra loads!

And of course, the BEST strategy is to

avoid adding to the pile in the first place.

Be on the look out:
STRESS comes in all shapes & sizes!

The next area focused on **MANAGING EMOTIONS.**

FEELINGS HAPPEN!

It is our job to become aware of them & manage them.

The key to remember here is:

Carol's Two Steps to Success!

Step 1) STOP the level from rising higher.

Step 2) RELEASE so the level will drop.

Don't talk until you've reached below neck level!

The last area we focused on: **THE POWER TOOLS.**

Once you can get your brain working
for you rather than against you –

YOU CAN ACCOMPLISH
ANYTHING!

Our thoughts & the words we choose to use
are the paint brushes we use to create our life!

If you take nothing else away from this chapter
I can only hope that it is how to use

One Day at A Time
&
The Serenity Prayer

One very important point to remember:

We CANNOT LET GO of anything

we

DON"T ALLOW OURSELVES TO FEEL!

 And in order to FEEL love, joy, happiness

we must also FEEL sadness, anger, pain

We can't separate the two sides of a coin!

One last **LIFETOOL:**

LifeTOOL #66

$$F_{ully}$$

$$E_{xamine}$$

$$E_{motional}$$

$$L_{essons}$$

I created a smaller book that contains just the tools!

This way you can have it always nearby,

to quickly reinforce the tools that work best for you!

A Caregiver's Toolbox:

Just the Tools from STRETCHED Not Broken!

Want to Speed Up Your Progress?

Master the Tools Even Faster!

 ## The
Tool Master

The Tool Master program provides you with **additional tools & training** to give you the *confidence* to successfully be managing your stress and your wellness!

This 4 Step System includes:

\# 1 – L.I.F.E. Wellness Blueprint (Value: $225)
\# 2 – The Feelings Pendulum (Value: $225)
\# 3 – Stress Away (Value: $225)
\# 4 – The Anger Umbrella (Value: $225)

Total Value: $ 900

Your investment: ~~$900~~ ~~$700~~ ~~$400~~

A special value awaits you at:

www.STRETCHEDnotBroken.com

About the Author

Carol has written over a dozen publications &
conducted national training on stress and wellness.

She is the founder and CEO of Well YOUniversity, LLC,
a global leader in health education & training,
whose mission is to empower individuals with
the tools and supports to achieve lifelong wellness.

Carol is a popular speaker / trainer at all types of
conferences and events. She provides community
education for hospitals, continuing education programs,
staff professional development and CEU/CME courses.

Her high energy, unique approach and compelling
presentation change thinking and inspire participants
to take action towards L.I.F.E wellness
(Living Intentionally & Fully Engaged).

Carol can be reached at Carol@WellYOUniversity.com.

Facebook: www.FaceBook.com/WellYOUniversity

Have Carol Speak at Your Next Event!

Get more information about how you can have Carol speak at your organization, event, or conference.

Go to: www.CarolLRickard.com

Or call: 888 Life Tools (543-3866)

Carol's Other Books

A Caregiver's Toolbox – Just the Tools!
(A smaller companion book to let you quickly access your tools)

Transforming Illness to Wellness

Emotional Eating

Putting Your Weight Loss on Auto

The Benefits of Smoking

Moving Beyond Depression

LifeTools

Words At Work Vol. 1

Words at Work Vol. 2

Creating Compliance (clinician's)

Relapse Prevention (clinician's)

Please visit us at:

www.WellYOUniversity.com

Sign up for weekly motivational e-quote!

Check out our upcoming FREE webinars!

Learn more about our training programs.

Email us your success story at:

Success@WellYOUniversity.com

CPSIA information can be obtained at www.ICGtesting.com
Printed in the USA
BVOW01s1853040816

457994BV00012B/74/P